I0441203

Emotional Intelligence

Emotional Intelligence

The right Behaviour to boost your Self Confidence, improve your Relationship and Influence People with the Emotions, Empath and Self Discipline.

Copyright © 2019 Daniel Stevens
All rights reserved.

Table of contents

INTRODUCTION

I bet if you were asked two decades ago what are the factors that determine a person's overall success in life, you would say a high intelligence quotient, good grades and well-developed cognitive functions. It was natural to assume that the ones with high intelligence in general were had higher chances of being successful. Parents and educators sang the same tune of high intelligence translating into greater success. Wish it was actually that simple!

If you want to be successful in life study hard, get awesome grades, go to college, study harder and graduate with really high honors – this was believed to be the sure shot highway to a great job and an abundantly successful life.

You spent years believing this notion and though it's not completely incorrect, it's not the full picture too! Success is a combination of several factors, the fundamental of them being your ability to handle your and other people's emotions.

Enter Emotional Intelligence or Emotional Quotient (both represent the same idea), which is a type of intelligence that determines an individual's ability to recognize and manage/control their and other people's emotions. It is a simple and straightforward concept that comprises two main components.

First, identifying or recognizing emotions, intentions, desires and goals in yourself and other people. Second, managing these emotions and actions to accomplish the most positive outcome for everyone involved.

Research on emotional intelligence has been ongoing since mid 20-th century within the psycho-scientific community. However, it wasn't until 1995, when Daniel Goleman published his book by the same name that emotional intelligence rolled into the mainstream consciousness and became a path-breaking concept.

Until then Intelligence Quotient was seen as clinching factor. Once emotional intelligence took over, IQ was looked upon as a narrow or limited way of assessing an individual's chances of success. The cut-throat world of career, jobs and business was seen as starkly different from the cushy confines of a classroom.

If one had to navigate the real world, they'd have to adapt to a different kind of intelligence than the academic one used in classrooms or libraries. A person's knowledge and cognitive abilities alone didn't guarantee success in life. A degree wasn't automatically going to convert into a high paying job or profitable business.

A best, you'll get your foot into the door. However, to sustain a person will need much more than plain intelligence. It will take social, communication, conversation and emotional skills to raise the bar. These are real life skills that don't come in the classroom but are learnt by living in a hostel, waiting at bars, joining social clubs, being a part of sports teams and volunteering.

You still think IQ is the only factor that determines a person's overall success in life? If that was true my friend, every successful person you spot today from the CEO of big organizations to the president to thought leaders to successful entrepreneurs should be a Harvard, Stanford, MIT PhD. Are they?

Make a list of 10 successful people you admire the most. They are one you look up to and think of as leading successful and balanced lives. Are all these folks top honors graduates from distinguished educational institutions with a high IQ? My money is on no!

Again, don't get me wrong here. I am not undermining the importance of intelligence or asking you to shut that book on mechanical engineering and start reading about human psychology. It is awesome if you posses naturally high cognitive abilities and a high Intelligence Quotient. All I am saying is, you should ideally have both EQ and IQ complementing each other to increase your chances of success in the real world. If you can increase your emotional quotient to back an already high intelligence quotient, you can create miracles!

However, if you ask me to pick between two skills, I would put my money on emotional intelligence. A person with average intelligence and highly evolved emotional intelligence has a greater chance of succeeding in today's world than a person with high intelligence and less developed emotional intelligence. The name of the game today is about managing people, understanding their emotions/ motives and managing their feelings to achieve the most positive results.

Technical knowledge may help you direct or instruct your team when it comes to demonstrating a task. However, your ability to keep them motivated by understanding their emotions will ensure if they'll stay inspired and productive throughout the process.

A person's cognitive intelligence or intellectual potential has always been measured as his/her ability to retain facts or make calculations. However, these skills aren't necessarily all-encompassing in certain positions such as leadership and entrepreneurship. Tons of CEOs, world leaders and Fortune 500 company founders are high-school dropouts. If intelligence alone was the measure of a person's success, how would you explain this?

The reality is that it isn't as straightforward as a single factor like intelligence determining our success. It in fact a combination of factors, predominantly emotional and social life skills that will help him survive or thrive in the real world. Intelligence quotient is an inborn but not all-inclusive factor influencing an individual's overall life success.

This is good news because irrespective of your traditional, genetically determined intelligence, you have a good chance of success if you work upon other social-emotional life skills. A high emotional quotient along with other social and psychological skill sets can boost your chances of success.

The objective of this book is to discuss crucial aspects of emotional intelligence and how to adopt them in your everyday life to increase your chances of success. We'll take a look at practical techniques to raise your emotional quotient and eventually boost your chances of success.

CHAPTER 1

EMOTIONAL INTELLIGENCE EXPLAINED

The term emotional intelligence and its more informal abbreviation EQ has gained some sort of cult, ubiquitous following in the self-development genre. Everyone from students to corporate professionals to government service personnel is waking up to the importance of boosting their emotional quotient or gaining greater awareness of their/other's emotions. Heck, even comic strips such as Dilbert feature the concept of emotional intelligent.

Have you seen one of those kid toy boxes that talk about how playing with xyz toy can boost your child's emotional intelligence? Or those personal ads that wax eloquence about how their prospective partner should be emotionally intelligent? There are quips printed on toiletry bottles too about emotional intelligence. So basically, it has become all-prevailing and tough to escape.

What exactly is emotional intelligence then? And why has it spread so rapidly into the mainstream culture?

The term emotional intelligence was first coined by two researchers – Peter Salavoy and John Meyer. However, it gained popularity only post the 1996 bestseller of the same name authored by renowned psychologist – Dan Goleman.

Emotional intelligence fundamentally comprises of identifying, understanding and effectively managing your own emotions, while also being able to recognize, comprehend, deal with and influence the emotions of other people for forging more harmonious relationships.

The concept of emotional intelligence has become so widespread that it has found a place in languages as diverse as Chinese, Malay, German, Malay and Portuguese. What's more? Even religious scholars across the world have woken up to the concept of emotional intelligence, and interweaved it into their faith.

How does emotional intelligence work in practical terms? Being aware of our emotions gives us the power to manage our behavior, and influence people positively. Learning to manage the behavior of other people can impact our relationships more positively.

Today some companies/corporate professionals accord emotional intelligence even more importance than traditional intelligence because it is considered an invaluable workplace asset. Many recruitment firms make emotional intelligence their clinching factor while deciding upon the successful candidate.

How do you pick between people who possess similar educational qualifications, skills, work experience and proficiency? All qualified candidates possess the knowledge and skills required for a job. What is it that differentiates you from a hundred other folks who've got the same set of skills, education background and experience as you?

Are you able to connect with people? Are you able to understand their emotions and work your way through it to get the best out of them? Are you able to manage your own emotions to optimize productivity? All things being equal, people with high emotional intelligence are almost always preferred over those that struggle with their/other's emotions.

Let us acquire a detailed overview of what emotional intelligence encompasses. Here are some major categories of emotional intelligence.

Self-Awareness

Self awareness is the ability to identify or label an emotion as it occurs in your mind. This is the cornerstone of emotional intelligence. You should be able to recognize your emotions to be able to manage them more effectively. If you fail to recognize that you are experiencing jealousy towards someone else, how will you deal with it? Tuning into your real feelings is at the base of emotional intelligence.

Once you are able to identify your emotions, and their consequences, it becomes easier to manage the effects of those emotions. This invariably boosts your confidence, and makes you more self-assured about your abilities. Self-awareness gives you a heightened sense of self-worth, self-confidence and self-esteem

Self Regulation

We don't have much control over how we experience and process emotions. However, the mind can be trained to control how long the impact of an emotion stays with you through a series of techniques. This simply gives you greater power to beat destructive emotions such as anxiety, depression, fear, anger and insecurity.

Self regulation can help manage disruptive impulses. It can also boost trustworthiness in relationships, helping you maintain higher standards of integrity, trust and honestly. It will help you develop a higher sense of conscientiousness or taking responsibility for your actions/results.

By learning to self-regulate emotions, we develop adaptability, flexibility and the ability to handle change more efficiently. It also paves the way for greater innovation, and the ability to be accepting of new ideas.

Motivation – Motivating yourself and others becomes a way of life when you are sport a more positive and emotionally balanced attitude. Although most people function with a predominantly negative or positive attitude, they can be trained to develop a more positive mindset with practice and dedication.

When you develop the ability of catching negative thoughts as they strike, you are able to quickly mould them into more positive constructive thoughts, which can help accomplish your goals.

Emotional intelligence can help boost your achievement drive, your sense of commitment, the ability to take initiative and optimism. When you're emotionally intelligent, you are ready to efficiently act upon the given opportunities. You're also more quipped to fulfill goals despite obstacles, challenges and setbacks.

Empathy

The ability to identify people's emotions is critical to success in both your personal and professional life. The more perceptive and discerning you are towards other's feelings, the better you can manage your behavior towards them.

A person high on empathy excels at preempting,

recognizing and meeting the needs of others (such a valuable asset when it comes to pleasing clients in corporate set-ups), developing other's abilities, leveraging diversity to create more opportunities, raising political awareness (understanding the emotional dynamics and power relationships of different groups), and developing a high understanding of the desires and needs of others to motivate them more efficiently.

Social Skills

Evolved interpersonal skills are the mainstay of a person's social, personal and business well-being. In today's hyper connected world, everyone had equal access to knowledge and technical resources.

If you're a programmer, differentiates you from thousands of other programmers who know coding at the back of their hand? If you're an experienced surgeon, what distinguishes you from other nifty surgeons who have performed thousands of surgeries?

When everyone possesses equal technical know-how, the only thing that differentiates one professional from another is his/her ability to connect with people. Thus people skills are given as much value today as technical expertise. A surgeon's ability to understand and empathize with his patient is today as important as his ability to perform skilled surgeries. People with a high emotional quotient are known to understand, lead, empathize, motivate and negotiate better with others in a fast-paced global economic environment.

Social tactics such as influencing others, wielding the power of persuasion, negotiating, communicating effectively, leading, being a change catalyst, managing conflict, building bonds, collaborating/co-operating, team work and more are easier to practice when you have a well-developed/nurtured emotional quotient.

Psychologists have agreed that only 10% of our success can be attributed to intelligence (not more than 25% at the most) quotient. The rest depends on several factors including the vital emotional intelligence. A revealing study conducted on Harvard graduates in several fields spanning medicine, law, teaching etc. demonstrated a zero and even negative correlation between success in the entrance test scores and success in their career. This clearly reveals that intelligence alone is clearly inefficient without emotional competencies, and that to experience holistic success in life we must be equipped to deal with our and other people's emotions.

The psychology of attachment states that all our current emotional experiences can be traced back to our early trysts with emotions. Your present day ability to cope with emotions such as unhappiness, anger, fear, and happiness in inextricably linked to nature of your early emotional experiences. If your emotions were acknowledged and valued in early stages, they can become invaluable life assets. Similarly, if the experiences were more painful and scary, you will most likely detach yourself from these emotions.

Emotional intelligence helps you connect with your emotions and identify changing feelings the moment they occur. This is critical to managing your thoughts and actions. Understanding our emotions is the key to managing them. This leads us to think logically about an emotion before acting upon it. We are no longer slaves of our impulses, and wield greater control on our actions on account of being more aware of our emotions. This prevents us from taking irrational and destructive steps that we end up regretting in hindsight.

You also learn the fine art of putting yourself in other's shoes by developing greater empathy. This can be a huge asset in your personal and business life. For instance, if an employee is not putting in his best, an emotionally intelligent person won't automatically assume he/she is being lazy or disinterested in working.

On the contrary, they will reach out to the person and examine his reasons for performing below his abilities. He may simply be afraid of making mistakes, or he may be low on self-confidence about his/her abilities. Problem resolution becomes much easier when you are able to put yourself in someone else's shoes, and feel things from their perspective.

Two people returned home post work after having a huge fight with their manager (let's call them Person A and Person B). Person A wasn't very emotionally intelligent. On returning home, he found his children playing noisily. His immediate reaction was to shout at the top of his voice and ask the children to shut up. He acted purely on his emotions which were misdirected form his manager to his children, who had nothing to do with him being upset. Person A didn't stop and think before acting on his emotions.

When Person B got home and discovered his children were playing noisily, he stepped back mentally and controlled his urge to scream by rationalizing that the children at nothing to do with the way he felt. Why then should they bear the brunt of his feelings? They weren't responsible for his emotions; therefore why make them face the consequences by yelling at them. The children always made a loud noise while playing, what's the point of gunning for them today just because I am upset with my manager?

Person B recognized that the main cause of him being in a foul mood was his boss, and therefore was able to act upon his emotions in a less impulsive and more rational manner. He displayed exemplary emotional intelligence.

Let's consider another example to strengthen your understanding of emotional intelligence. Say you've been assigned an extremely prestigious project. Your manager is putting you under a lot of pressure to do it really well. You are aware there are plenty of co-workers who'd be ready to take over the project from you without batting an eyelid. How does a person deal with such a stressful situation?

There are two main options when it comes to reacting to such a situation. You can buckle under the pressure of losing a vital project because human beings are essentially wired for reacting on emotions first without thinking their decisions through. Alternatively a person with high emotional intelligence can use this stress as a motivator to perform above expectations, and use the opportunity to come out tops in the eyes of the management.

The emotionally intelligent person may feel slightly overwhelmed initially; however he/she will quickly gather themselves and get to work by finding their inner bearings. Not only are such folks able to balance themselves more efficiently but they can also utilize stress as fantastic motivation means.

How do people react when they are offered feedback, even of the more positive and constructive kind? People with low emotional intelligence will come up with a bundle of excuses to hide their shortcomings or short of expectations performance. They may shy away from acknowledging their mistakes or make someone else the scapegoat for their inefficiency. They will take the shorter route of snapping by giving into their emotions rather than taking the time to think it through. It's easier to simply give in to your emotions, but recognizing and controlling them takes effort.

On the other hand, a person with higher emotional

intelligence will accept that they aren't perfect. Instead of taking the feedback personally, they'll delve deeper into themselves to work out what went wrong, and avoid making the same mistakes in future. They will listen intently, and focus on the developing themselves rather than worrying about being right all the time. Emotionally intelligent folks are less likely to argue, retort and throw accusations. They will be more open to suggestions and constructive feedback, which will help them reach their goals.

They will listen and absorb the information, and work on it. For them, it's more about developing themselves than being right or wrong. They will even thank the person for giving feedback for his/her inputs.

Let's consider another example of emotional intelligence. You are engaged in a discussion about politics with a friend. You are expressing your personal political views/beliefs, while he/she is vocalizing his/her ideas. You sense a more angry tone when they talk about their beliefs. Since you are clued in to their emotions, you realize that the topic is slightly sensitive and may upset them.

You quickly take a grip of the situation and understand gently acknowledge their view, even if you do not agree with it. Since you were more sensitive and thoughtful to your classmate's feelings through non-verbal clues and physical reactions, you were able to diffuse a potentially volatile situation respectfully, thus ending things on a more positive note.

Imagine a scenario where you weren't emotionally intelligent or thoughtful towards the other person's emotions. You would have simply stuck to a view that would've fanned their flaming emotions even more, thus snowballing into a situation where everyone ends up hurt and upset, and the situation ends negatively, thus impacting your interpersonal relationship.

Almost all of us know an emotionally intelligent person (if you're lucky, more than one maybe). He/she always seems to be saying the right things, however tricky the situation. They have a way of "handling the situation" and preventing it from becoming negative/destructive. They know how to assert themselves without offending others. These folks are also more caring, sensitive, considerate, compassionate and empathetic.

They don't allow emotions to swing their behavior. Emotionally intelligent people may not have the answers to all your problems but they have the ability to make you feel more positive and hopeful about a situation.

According to research conducted by Dr. Travis Bradberry, 90% of top performing personnel in any organization have a high emotional quotient, 58% of your job performance is a result of emotional intelligence and that people with high emotional intelligence make $29,000 more annually than their low emotional intelligence professional counterparts. Thus people with high emotional quotient not perform well, but also earn more on an average than those with low emotional quotient.

What is the Difference Between IQ and EQ?

Intelligence Quotient and Emotional Quotient both determine intelligence, albeit different types of intelligence. While IQ is a measure of a person's cognitive abilities, EQ measures his/her emotional intelligence.

All the technical skills you've studied and practically learnt contribute towards your intelligence quotient. They may you technically competent, and determine your success when it comes to performing the actual job.

However, in today's dynamic and socially charged world, intelligence alone does not determine one's success. You must also learn the art of managing your own and other's emotions to be able to develop optimally productive and fulfilling relationships. Unless you live in a cardboard box all by yourself, emotional intelligence is a necessity to be able to deal with people around you.

Imagine being in charge of one of the most prestigious projects your organization could bag. You've been given an extremely talented, skilled and experienced team to helm the project. However, the project involved hours and hours of additional work, lots of back-breaking research and sometimes working on weekends too. As someone who is proficient in his/her task, you're capable of leading from the front.

However, since it's such a high pressure and stressful

project, are you able to persuade your team to put in extra effort and stay motivated throughout the project? Your technical prowess will help them gain the right skills; however, it is your emotional intelligence quotient which will help you keep your team inspired, positive, efficient and productive. The way you deal with your and their emotions will determine to a large extent how they perform under a high pressure situation.

While your technical skills are a direct result of your intelligence and ability, your ability to manage the team's behavior is influenced by your emotional quotient. By gaining a more evolved understanding of your team's feelings, passions, motivators and behavior, you can manage their actions for optimum productivity.

It is easier to get people to do what you want them to (in a good way unlike negative manipulation) when you gain insights into their emotional behavior. What is it that drives them? Some people react better to heaps of appreciation than monetary incentives, while others dig being applauded publically. What leads people to behave the way they do? If a particular worker is always drawing attention to himself/herself, he she may be suffering from low self esteem issues. When you understand the underlying emotions behind their behavior pattern, it becomes easier to manage their actions. This is the basic difference between emotional quotient and intelligence quotient.

Notice how wonderfully politicians, leaders, advertisers

and other mass communicators use the power of emotional intelligence to create popular opinion? Or how they influence/persuade the masses to make decisions to their advantage?

Brands and advertising agencies are forever harnessing the power of emotions such as fear, happiness and aspirations to impact the buying behavior of their target audience. They use the emotional behavior of their target audience to their advantage by creating clever promotional messages that quickly urge people to take action.

Emotional quotient, unlike intelligence quotient, dips into the most basic emotions that influence our actions or behavior pattern. While your IQ stays more or less the same at 15 and 65, EQ is more dynamic. It can be cultivated with a little training, practice and experience. Emotional intelligence is more flexible and evolving.

Individuals having a high IQ are awesome at completing cognitive tasks. They are capable of learning and absorbing skills/information rather quickly. However, if the same high IQ people have a low emotional quotient, they will find it challenging to recognize their and other people's feelings, thus being unable to manage these emotions effectively. If things don't turn out according to their expectations, these individuals are prone to anger fits or lashing out at others without considering their feelings. They don't get along well with people and generally struggle with social adaptability.

Emotional intelligence has acquired a huge momentum in the last couple of decades, and has permeated into several areas including sports, government agencies and the corporate world.

A majority of conflicts in personal relationships are a direct result of low emotional intelligence or the ability to connect to the other person's internal feelings.

Brief History of Emotional Intelligence

The ground or brief foundation for the concept of emotional quotient or intelligence was first laid in 1983 by Harvard professor and psychologist Howard Gardner in his "Theory of Multiple Intelligences." The paper spoke about different kinds of intelligences that impact our lives. It put forth the theory of interpersonal intelligence as one's ability to recognize motivations, desires, intentions and needs of other people.

The study also spoke about intrapersonal intelligence which reflected an individual's ability to identify his/her deepest emotions, triggers, fears and motivations. The study set the ball rolling for what's now become a huge psychological concept connected to helping people gain a better understand of their and other people's emotions.

Emotional intelligence as a term was originally coined by researchers-professors John D. Meyer and Peter Salovey in the early 90's. They referred to it as a kind if social intelligence which awards people the knack for recognizing their and other people's emotions, which in turn is effective in guiding their actions.

Though it was this duo that first coined the term and introduced the concept, it was Daniel Goleman who made the concept of emotional intelligence a rage with 1990 book Emotional Intelligence. Goleman was a journalist who specialized in writing about behavior sciences and popular psychology for publications such as the New York Times. He worked closely with several behavioral specialists such as David McClelland.

McClelland along with a group of other research colleagues was looking for alternatives for standard IQ tests, given the fact that these tests didn't reveal much about the qualities that are needed to be successful in life.

While looking around for studies for his publication on emotions, Goleman came across Salovey and Mayer's study. He then went ahead and sought permission from these experts for utilizing the term "emotional intelligence" in the book he was authoring. Originally the publication was supposed to be a discussion along the lines of "emotional literacy", the focus quickly changed to emotional intelligence as a result of Salovey-Mayer's study.

Goleman staunchly believed that cognitive intelligence alone contributed little to a person's overall success. He underlined the relevance of emotional intelligence that gave people the ability to understand their emotions, managing their emotions, identify other's emotions and handle them effectively by displaying high social skills.

Goleman's books endorsed the concept of emotional intelligence as even more important than IQ to determine our success in life. The idea of EQ became so revolutionary that Goleman's book ended up selling a staggering 5 million copies within half a decade. The world welcomed emotional quotient with open arms and lapped it up for living more gratifying and fulfilled lives.

Though the book discussed the concept of emotional intelligence in depth, it offered little in terms of helping readers increase their emotional quotient.

How Can Emotional Intelligence Affect Your Daily Life?

1. Emotional intelligence helps you negotiate the social complexities in your school, university and workplace. It not just helps in leading and motivating others, but also gives you the right disposition to excel at work. Like we discussed earlier, several recruitment firms now conduct emotional intelligence tests for gauging a person's emotional and social adaptability before hiring. Emotional intelligence can help you do your best in school and work.

2. Your physical health is more or less a result of your inability to cope with stress. High stress can lead to health issues such as an inefficient immune system, high blood pressure, increased risk of heart ailments, infertility and faster aging. One of the biggest consequences of boosting

your emotional intelligence is decrease in stress.

When you are able to identify your and other people's emotions more effectively, it leads to less stressful situations. Conflict management and differences are easier to resolve. You are better adjusted and adapted to the person around you, which leads to fewer opportunities for stressful situations.

This is easy to understand. When we are emotionally happy and well-adjusted, it shows on our body. People with a high emotional quotient are capable of managing their emotions better to cope with issues such as anxiety and stress more positively. They don't stress over what is beyond their circle of influence, but instead control what they can. This leads emotionally intelligent folks to sport better physical health and over all well-being.

3. Negative emotions when not controlled at the right time can snowball into mental health issues such as anxiety, panic attacks and depression. When you struggle with the ability to manage your and other people's emotions, you are more vulnerable to feeling isolated, depressed and lonely. Emotional intelligence allows you to develop a greater understanding towards people and situations, thus leading to lower stress and better mental health.

4. When you understand your emotions, and learn how to manage them, you can express yourself even more

effectively. Similarly, when you understand the feelings of others, it is easier to reach out to them in a constructive and positive manner. This helps you communicate efficiently with people to build stronger and more meaningful relationships.

Let's take an example to understand how emotional intelligence impacts our relationships. Person X and Y are deeply involved in a romantic relationship. However, they are both as different and chalk and cheese. While X is outgoing and social, Y is more reserved, reticent and selective (when it comes to making friends). Y doesn't understand why X needs to spend so much time with friends.

If X doesn't have a high emotional quotient, he/she will be prone to labeling Y as an insecure and over-possessive partner, thus creating conflict within the relationship. Y will get defensive in the face of X's accusations. However if X is emotionally intelligent, he/she be able to understand and empathize with Y. He/she will try to gather why Y feels the way he/she does. He/she will try to involve B more in their social outings, and make Y feel an important part of the group. X will take constructive steps that will benefit both of them, and work out a sort of understanding to reduce conflict.

X will gently explain to Y about why he/she needs some time off with friends without arguing or blaming Y. There is a greater attempt to reach out to the other person and work out a middle ground that benefits everyone. In the above example, X may make more time for Y on weekends, while partying with his/her friends on other days. X has simply utilized his knowledge and understanding of Y's emotions to work out a solution where everyone is happy, and which allows them both to enjoy a more meaningful and gratifying relationship.

In the above scenario, A may keep aside some days exclusively for B, while working out a way to go out with friends once a week so B doesn't feel neglected. This way, A has used his knowledge of B's emotions and feelings to empathize with her and arrive at a solution that makes them both feel better, which allows them to share a more meaningful and fulfilling relationship.

CHAPTER 2

PROVEN STRATEGIES FOR BOOSTING SELF AWARENESS AND MANAGING EMOTIONS

People with greater emotional self-awareness are aware about their feelings at any point in time. They can identify the exact source of those emotions, and can also contemplate how these emotions will be manifested in physical form such as headaches, faster heart beat and sweaty palms. Now that you know what self-awareness is and how it can benefit you, wouldn't you want to know how to build greater self-awareness?

The first step towards developing greater emotional intelligence is boosting self-awareness or your understanding of your own feelings and emotions. You can regulate your emotions for an optimally positive outcome only when you are able to identify these emotions. Labeling emotions and them determining your actions based on these emotions is critical to the process of developing emotional intelligence.

When you are more aware of your feelings and emotions, recognizing other people's emotions becomes simpler. Here are solid, proven tips for boosting self-awareness to get you started on the path of emotional intelligence.

1. Be An Authority On Yourself

What is the first step when you aim to bring about changes in your thoughts, actions and behavior? Awareness about these thoughts and subsequent actions! To make changes, you ought to know what you have to improve upon.

Knowing yourself inside out is the key to being more emotionally aware and savvy. Did you know athletes are trained to identify and overcome feelings before an important upcoming game? This is based on the premise that if you can successfully identify and control your emotions, it doesn't impact your productivity.

Go back and think about all the recent instances where you let emotions get the better of you and affect your productivity. Haven't you let trivial matters impact your performance?

When you are aware of your strengths and weaknesses, it is easier to confidently accomplish your objectives. There is a lesser scope for frustration, unproductivity and disappointment. Self confidence increases your assertiveness while expressing thoughts and opinions, which is important for developing social skills.

When you gain greater awareness, you will rarely be ruled by emotions. You have a clear edge if you are able to regulate your emotions. An emotionally aware person stops being a victim of his emotions and in fact uses these emotions in a positive way to accomplish the desired outcome.

Spend time recognizing areas of development to strengthen it.

- List all your strengths and weaknesses.

- Take a formal, psychological personality assessment test that helps you discover your own skills, abilities, limitations and values.

- Obtain objective feedback from people you trust.

One way that works wonders for increasing your self-awareness is journaling. Write in a flowing stream of consciousness about the thoughts you are feeling and experiencing as they are occurring. What are the emotions you are experiencing? What are the physiological reactions to your feelings? Are you experiencing a faster heartbeat, sweaty palms, increased pulse etc. as a physical reaction to your emotions?

Emotions aren't always straightforward. In fact, they are complex and multi-layered. For example, you may have a heated argument with your partner and feel angry, hurt, upset, vengeful, all at the same time. Write emotions exactly as you are experiencing them, even if two emotions appear to contradict each other. For instance, if you've got a scholarship to study overseas, you may be elated at the opportunity. However, the thought of leaving behind your partner may cause tinges of sadness too. You are acknowledging and validating your emotions by writing them.

Dexter Valles, the CEO of Valmar International suggests maintaining a whiteboard divided into two to three parts throughout the day. Add six to eight feelings to the board and ask employees to tick against the feelings they experience at different points during the day. Determine which emotions have the maximum check marks.

Make a list of every role you play in your daily life such as a parent, sibling, volunteer, worker and more. What are the emotions liked with each role? For example, you may enjoy your role as a parent but may be an unhappy employee. Examine every role and the emotions attached to it carefully.

Naming emotions linked to every relationship will help

you manage emotions within that relationship more efficiently. It will keep you in greater control of your emotional reaction where the specific role is concerned.

2. Do a Periodic Mental Check-in

It's like the guest services/housekeeping staff knocking on your room and checking in if you need something all the time. You do a mental check by peeping into your mind throughout the day to understand if it's doing fine or needs something.

Set aside some time each day to take a stock of your feelings. You can simply answer questions such as how are you feeling at that particular moment? What is the source of those feelings? What are the physical symptoms of these feelings? Are you experiencing tensed shoulders? Clenched teeth? Fear, joy, excitement, sadness, euphoria?

Do your feelings/emotions flow quickly one after another? Are your feelings accompanied by marked physical sensations, especially in the chest and stomach? Are emotions such as anger, sadness, happiness and fear evident through your facial expressions? Are your feelings intense enough to grab the attention of others? Do your emotions determine your decisions?

If these experiences do not ring a bell with you, your emotions may most likely be tuned off. To be emotionally balanced and intelligent, you must be able to reconnect with your fundamental emotions, acknowledge them, accept these emotions, and befriend them.

3. Name Your Emotions

Label and categorize your emotions. I know this makes your feelings sound like they belong to a library. However, labeling or giving names to your emotions makes it easier to identify and act upon them. When you feel an emotion surging through you, attempt to identify it quickly. Is it fear, insecurity, jealousy, anger, elation, depression, surprise or a combination of these emotions?

Identify the triggers that cause these emotions. For instance, a specific person my evoke jealousy in your because you feel they are more successful than you.

What leads to feel certain emotions? What are the triggers that anger or hurt you? What makes you happy and sad? What is the source of positive and destructive emotions in you? Labeling your feelings and recognizing the stimuli for various emotions will increase your emotional self-awareness.

Grab a pen and paper to list your emotion when you experience a compelling feeling. Mention the precise emotion or feeling you are experiencing. Accompany this emotional label with the trigger that caused it. What is leading you to feel the way you do? When you recognize an emotion, it is easier to manage it.

For instance, let us assume you feel a deep sense of loathing for a person without any specific reason. You dislike them and can't stand them, but funnily can't tell why you dislike them. On closer examination of your feelings, you realize you dislike them because you are envious of them. You may believe they are always having a wonderful life, while things never go your way. When you are able to nail this emotion as jealousy, you are more equipped to regulate you potentially negative emotions.

Once you recognize the emotion as irrational jealousy, you will view it in a more logical and understanding manner. You'll begin to think along the lines that it isn't really someone's fault that they lead an amazing life. In fact, they should be applauded for working hard towards their goals. You'll realize that no one has a perfect life. Everyone goes through shares of trials and tribulation to attain success, which isn't necessarily visible to the outside world. Sometimes, it is only how we perceive things and not the reality. Thus, once you are more mindful of your emotions, you can work with them more positively.

4. Mindfulness

Tune in to what your feelings and emotions are trying to convey to you during any moment. Develop a connection with your inner self or intuition to know what it's telling you about how you are feelings. When you "|listen to"| your deepest feelings, you gain invaluable insights about your emotional experiences, which guide you in handling several problems and issues.

Staying in the moment is one of the best ways for recognizing emotions as they happen. Get rid of the habit of rehashing or replaying past stressful situations in your mind. If the problem isn't resolved yet, try coming up with out of the box solutions at present rather than spending energy focusing on where you went wrong in the past. Shift the focus form what you can't control to what you can.

Practice meditation and deep breathing to improve self-awareness and emotional intelligence. Meditation helps in calming your thoughts or taming the mind. It helps you develop greater awareness about your thoughts.

Taking a few deep breaths helps your brain collect a fresh supply of oxygen, which can award more clarity to your thinking and make you feel less stressed.

Emotionally intelligent folks spend plenty of time building self-awareness. They meditate or reflect upon their actions daily. Devote some time from your busy schedule to meditation and reflection, which will ultimately help you connect with yourself and build greater self-awareness. Head to any quiet corner within your home or office, and spend time on any activity that gets you in touch with your deeper, inner self.

Try doing this simple deep breathing exercise. Breathe in at the count of 1, and then breathe out at the count of 1. Slower the paces a bit by breathing it at the count of 1-2, then breathe out at the count of 1-2. Make the pace even more relaxed by breathing in at the count of 1-3, followed by breathing out at the count of 1-3. Finally, count from 1-4 while breathing in, and 1-4 while breathing out. Repeat the sequence as many times are you're comfortable with. Rest your hands on your chest or stomach to experience the rising and drowning of every breath.

Mindfulness is a fundamentally a Buddhist practice about channelizing all your attention on the present without judgment. While the roots of mindfulness can be traced back to Buddhism, almost every religion practices mindfulness through prayer or meditation.

It is all about appreciating the present moment without diving into the past or future. It is about developing a more calm and focused mindset that helps you make decisions with greater clarity. It is about carefully tuning in to every physical or emotional sensation, and gaining a bigger life perspective.

Mindfulness can bring about a deep sense of calmness, which can help you indentify your feelings objectively, and subsequently manage them. It helps you stay completely in the moment in a non-judgmental manner to get a better grip of your emotions before you are tempted to react to it.

It can be practiced just about anywhere and not just during meditation. For instance, you can practice mindful eating or mindful walking. Watch your emotions while eating or taking a long walk alone.

5. Get Feedback

You can solicit honest views from family, friends and trusted associates by clearing the ground at the outset by saying something like, "I am seeking your opinion as a friend, however be honest about this with me since I need a genuinely unbiased perspective. Alright?"

Another brilliant strategy is to get friends to call out when they see you doing something which you genuinely want to give up. For instance, "I like to hijack every conversation like you are aware by now, please do me a small favor and let me know gently each time I try to do that- discreetly if possible". They will gently nudge you to stop when you do something you want to change about yourself.

You must also seek to obtain an unbiased feedback at work. Use formal channels to get your supervisors/managers to offer you a formal and constructive feedback. It will allow you to dive into your strengths and weaknesses to increase your emotional intelligence and social adaptability. Seek a 360-feedback that offers you an unbiased opinion across several competency areas.

The journey of self-awareness is a never ending one. It is an evolving process that seeks to help gain complete congruence or consistency in the way to speak, think and act. You can never really be done with "being self aware". However the above mentioned techniques will help you take the highway or fast track to self-awareness.

Be Receptive to feedback and constructive criticism. One

of the best ways to develop greater awareness of your emotions is to be more open to feedback and criticism from others. For instance, a friend may tell you that each time he/she talks about his/her accomplishments; he/she senses your pangs of envy or dislike towards him/her. This may help you tune in to your emotions and emotional triggers more effectively.

Emotionally intelligent folks are open to receiving feedback and considering the other person's point of view. You may not necessarily agree with them, but listening to other people's criticism and feedback helps you work on your blind spots. This can help you recognize your thoughts, triggers and behavior patterns.

I know a person who in a bid to increase his self-awareness and emotional quotient actively goes around asking people for feedback about his words, feelings (as they understand it) and actions. It acts as a emotion-meter, which helps him gain greater awareness of his emotions and regulate them more efficiently.

6. Use Third Person

Research in the field of labeling our emotions has indicated that when we distance ourselves from our emotions or view them more objectively, we gain higher self-awareness. Next time you feel the urge is so, "I am disappointed" say "Jack is disappointed".

If that seems too preposterous, try saying, "I am presently

experiencing sadness" or "one of my feelings at the moment is sadness".

These are techniques through which you are distancing yourself from overpowering emotions to stay naturally composed. You are basically treating your emotions as just another piece of information rather than being overwhelmed by them.

Each time you find yourself experiencing an urge to react to a situation, take a moment to name it. Then use it in third person to distance yourself from intense emotions.

7. Do Not Attempt To Fix Emotions

You don't always have to identify emotions with the intention of fixing them. Self-awareness is not about fixing emotions. It is to recognize these emotions and allow them to pass rather than helping him get the better of you. Society has conditioned us to think of certain emotions are bad. We mistakenly believe that experiencing these emotions makes us a bad person.

Far from it, emotions aren't good or bad. They are just that – emotions. There's no need to push away the seemingly bad emotions. Acknowledge that you are experiencing an emotion by saying something like, "I am experiencing jealousy". Practice deep breathing for a while until the emotion passes. Rather than pushing the emotion away and in the process increasing its intensity to come back even stronger, gently acknowledge and let it live its time before passing away.

It takes around six seconds for the body to absorb emotion related chemicals. Give your body that much time.

We often share a hostile relationship with our emotions. They are believed to be something that is negative and should be fought or suppressed. However, emotions are information that helps us function in our daily lives. Overcome the mindset that emotions are good or bad, and instead focus on using them to empower you. Rather than letting emotions take control of you, use emotional information to work with them.

Emotions are neural hormones that are released as a direct response to our perceptions regarding the world. The direct us towards a specific action. All emotions have a distinct message and objective, which means there's nothing like a good or bad emotion.

For example, fear helps us focus on an impending danger and take the necessary action to defend ourselves. Similarly, sadness makes us experience a sense of loss and facilitates a better understanding of what we truly care about.

If you move away from your best friend and become sad, you truly care about him/her to experience sadness on moving away from him or her. This is valuable information. Hence, sadness is not a bad emotion. It can be used to identify what you care about.

If you use emotions as information for recognizing

feelings, they can be channelized positively. The number one rule for developing higher emotional intelligence is to stop judging and curbing your emotions.

8. Recognize Emotions Based on Physiological Reactions

Our emotions are often experienced within the physical body. For example, you may feel anxious before a job interview or important presentation. There may be "butterflies in your stomach" before addressing an audience on the stage.

Don't you find your heart pounding with excitement when you are about to go on a date with someone you've fancied for long? Nervousness leaves us with sweaty palms and stiff muscles.

While these are only some of the physiological reactions we experience, research has proven that a variety of emotions are strongly associated with activating certain parts within the body.

Regular patterns of physical sensations are linked with each of the six fundamental emotions including fear, happiness, anger, sadness, disgust and surprise. Human emotions discreet overlap physiological sensations. For example, reduced limb sensations are associated with sadness. Similarly, increased upper limb sensations are connected with anger. A strong feeling of disgust generates sensations within the throat and digestive system. Fear and surprise generate sensations within the chest.

9. Pin Down Recurring Patterns

This can be one of the most effective parts of knowing your-self. Neuroscience will help you understand the process more effectively. Our brains have an inherent tendency to follow established neural paths rather than creating new ones. This doesn't necessarily mean that the established patterns are serving us positively or that they can't be altered.

For instance, when a person becomes angry, he or she may bottle up their emotions rather than expressing it. This has become an emotional pattern with the person and is dee-ply embedded into the mind. However, awareness of this pattern can help the person chart another path of action, where the person practices responding instead of simply reacting to the emotion. However, the first step to charting a new pattern is identifying a pattern.

Recognize the build-up of emotions before something sud-denly triggers you. These triggers have a predictable pat-tern. If you are already frustrated, you are likelier to see a situation in a more negative light. Similarly, if you are over-come by fear, you are likelier to interpret a stimulus as the-reat. It is therefore important to be aware of these biases and how they can impact our emotions by creating a predi-ctable pattern. The more efficient you become in recogni-zing your biases, the lower will be your chances of misin-terpreting a stimulus.

10. Work With Available Information on Emotions

Emotions are important pieces of data that help you gauge things from a clearer and objective perspective. When you stop taking it suppress it, ignore it, fight or feel overwhelmed by it, we build a valuable library of emotions. The purpose of emotional awareness is to concentrate our attention on these emotions and use them positively to create the desired outcome not to curb them.

Treat your emotions as data that relies on your view about the world or about how to act. When you open yourself to this data, you enjoy access to a huge resource of emotions that can be utilized to drive you actions in the right direction. You will know exactly how to reach where you want to go if you have a clear emotional route map. Therefore acknowledge and recognize your emotions as data, and work with it rather than trying to beat it.

Begin by carefully noticing how you feel at the moment. Observe emotions without judging them or attempting to fix them. Learn to simply notice your emotions.

CHAPTER 3

POWERFUL VERBAL AND NON-VERBAL CLUES FOR BOOSTING EMOTIONAL INTELLIGENCE

When you are able to tune in to other people's emotions or empathize with how they feel, there is higher chance of responding appropriately to create the desired positive result. Thus our ability to connect with our and other people's emotions can be a powerful tool in social and leadership situations.

Understanding other people, helping overcome stress situations, motivating your team, negotiating business deals and building a close knit social circle becomes easier when you are able to leverage emotional information available about people. It increases situation awareness and our ability to read people, thus helping us make the most positive decision.

Here are some verbal and non verbal factors impacting social emotional quotient or our ability to read and deal with people.

Body Language

Research reveals that body language accounts for 50 percent of our communication. You'd wonder why there were words in the first place with body language accounting for half our communication process. Tuning in to a person's body language will help you pick up important signals related to their emotional state and subconscious thoughts/feelings.

Here's quick cue sheet to reading people's feelings through their body language.

- Crossed arms and legs are signals of people creating a subconscious barrier. They are emotionally closed, suspicious or do not subscribe to your ideas. They aren't open to listening to your views or disinterested in the topic of conversation. You may have to emotionally open the person up a bit by changing the topic and then get back to the original topic. The physical act of un-crossing their arms and legs will make them more sub-consciously receptive to your ideas.

- How can you tell a genuine smile from a fake one? Simple, it's all in the eyes. Observe it there's crink-led skin near the person's eyes forming crow's feet. People often present a happy expression to hide their true feelings. However, if their smile doesn't cause the skin around their eyes and mouth to crinkle, they are not most likely not as happy as they are pretending to be. Artificial smiles create wrinkles only around the mouth, while genuine smiles create wrinkles around the sides of the eyes.

- When people constantly take their gaze away from you while speaking, they are most likely not being very ho-nest or trying to hide something. Similarly, if a person speaks to you without taking their gaze away from you for long, they may be trying to threaten or intimidate you with their gaze. It is alright to look away periodi-cally. However, shifting gaze constantly is a red flag.

- When you are addressing a group of people, closely ob-serve the ones who are nodding excessively or in a more exaggerated manner. These are the people who are most concerned about your approval. They are anxious about making a positive impression and keen to be in your "good books."

- People who are nervous or anxious tend to fidget with their hands or objects. Other signs of nervousness also include excessive blinking, tapping feet and constantly running one's hand over the face.

- When an entire group walks into the room, how do you analyze who the leader or decision maker is? Quickly observe everyone's posture. The leader will most likely walk with a straight posture, with shoulders pulled out. Subconsciously, they are trying to occupy maximum space to convey authority over their team. Standing straight and pulling back shoulders increases a person's physical frame. It makes them come across as much bigger than they actually are, which is why people in power love to keep this posture to reveal their influence over a group or place.

- Expressions are windows of a person's emotional state. When a person is amazed or surprised, their eyebrows raise and the upper eyelids widen. Similarly, the mouth gapes open. Expressions can often overlap, so watch for microexpressions that can reveal precise emotions. For instance, raised eyebrows can also reveal fear. Look for other microexpresison clues to determine the exact emotion. If a person is experiencing fear, the eyebrows will be raised and pulled together with tensed lower eyelids, while the two corners of their lips will appear stretched. Similarly, surprise will be expressed by eyebrows pulled up and a lowered jaw. Learn to read the entire face, especially microexpressions if you want to learn more about how a person is feeling. Since microexpressions occur in a fraction of seconds, they are virtually impossible to fake. For instance, notice how when people are being deceptive, their mouths will assume a slanting position. Similarly, their eye movements become more rapid, the nostrils flare slightly and they purse their lip together (a subconscious gesture signaling their lips are sealed or they won't reveal the truth). Since these split expressions are so subconscious driven or involuntary, it is almost impossible to manipulate them. Enlarged pupils reveal intense emotions such as excitement, elation, delight, surprise and interest. When a person is attracted to you or truly delighted to see you, their pupils will involuntarily enlarge.

- The direction of a person's feet can also determine what's going on in their mind. Since feet aren't the first thing on anyone's mind, it harder to manipulate body language related to legs and feet. If a person's feet are pointing away from you, they are subconsciously signaling their need to escape. However, if the feet are pointed towards you, they are interested or in agreement with what you are saying.

- Typical signs of frustration and stress are clenched jaws, wrinkled eyebrows and tensed neck. The person's words notwithstanding, if you observe any of these, signs, he/she may be undergoing a stressful situation that they are trying to conceal. The trick for reading people's emotions accurately is to keep an eye out for a clear mismatch between verbal and non-verbal clues.

- Observe a person's walk to tune in to their feelings. People with a heavier gait along with low gravity while moving their legs are most likely hurt, stressed, frustrated or depressed. People who walk with a slower and more relaxed pace are reflecting upon something. Notice how confident, happy and goal-oriented people walk swiftly in one direction.

- Observing a person's eye movements is a near accurate way of gauging of how he or she is feeling, since our eye movements are connected to precise brain functions. Our eye movements have an established pattern depending on the brain function or type of information we are trying to access. For example, when a person is caught in an internal conflict or dilemma (to speak the truth or lie), they are likelier to look in the direction of their left collar bone. Darting eyes laterally from one side to another can be a deception red flag.

- Proxemics is a sub topic within body language that talks about how people reveal their feelings and emotions through the physical distance they maintain with other people during the process of face to face interaction or communication.

It is a powerful non verbal signal for understanding a person's thought process or state of mind. Psychologists and body language experts believe that the amount of physical distance we maintain while interacting with a person helps establish the dynamics of our relationship with them or reveals our emotions about them. A person who isn't standing very close to you may not be emotionally open or receptive to you. They may have a tendency to closely guard their emotions or give only a little of themselves to the interaction. Such people may be more emotionally guarded and closed. You may need to make extra effort to get them to drop their guard and feel less intimidated. It may be a defense mechanism against being emotionally hurt or vulnerable. On the other hand, if a person is leaning in your direction, they may subconsciously convey being emotionally open or trusting you with their feelings. They may also be more interested in what you are speaking about.

Tone

The tone, volume, pitch and emphasis of a person's voice can help you decode a lot about how they are feeling. For example, if you notice plenty of inconsistencies in the tone of their voice while speaking, they are probably very angry, hurt, excited or nervous. Ever notice how your voice shakes when you speak in a rage or are nervous about something? It can also be a sign the person is lying.

Similarly, if a person is speaking louder or softer than their regular volume, something may be amiss. Again, a person's tone is a dead giveaway. Sometimes people say something that sounds like a compliment. However, on examining their tone closely, you realize the sarcasm and feelings with which it was uttered.

The tone with which an individual completes their sentence says a lot about what they are trying to convey even with similar verbal clues. For example, if a person completes their sentence on a raised note, they are doubtful of something or inuring/asking a question. Similarly, if the finish the sentence is a flat tone, they are pronouncing a statement or judgment. Watch out for how people end their sentences to gather a clue into their inner feelings.

Again, the words people emphasize on can help you uncover their true feelings. For example, if a person says, "have you borrowed the blazer?" while emphasizing on "borrowed", it indicates their doubt over whether you have borrowed, stolen or done something else to the blazer. However, if the emphasis is on "you" they aren't sure if it is you or someone else who has borrowed the blazer.

I also like to look at pauses between phases to know about the person's attitude, emotions and intentions. For example, if a person pauses after saying something, it may that what they just said is extremely important to them or they truly believe in it. Sometimes, a person pauses to seek validation or feedback from others. The speaker wants to gauge your reaction to what they said since it is important for them.

When people are in a more emotionally unstable or negative frame of mind (angry hurt or upset), their voice tends to be more high pitched or squeaky. They may most likely be losing a grip of their emotions or aren't able to regulate their emotions effectively. Notice how when people are very angry, their voice becomes more screechy and squeaky, as if they are about to cry.

Speed Speech

A person's emotions clearly impact the speed of their speech. Notice how you start talking much faster than your normal rate of speech or words/minute when you are angry or upset. A rapid speech can convey lack of organization, uncertainty or lack of clarity. The person is not very comfortable about speaking, and is just trying to finish throwing his/her words. Again, a slower than usual pace translates into low self-confidence, inability to expression emotions, inability to come to terms with one's emotions, lack of emotional reassurance and other similar feelings.

Verbal Clues

A person's choice of words can say a lot about what they are thinking and feeling. Words are symbolic or our thoughts and feelings, which when combined with non verbal clues, give us a comprehensive understanding of their emotional state.

The human brain is a miracle really. When we think or process rational/logical thoughts, we tend to use nouns and verbs. Conversely, when we attempt to express our thoughts or feelings in a verbal or written format, there is a tendency to use more adverbs and adjectives.

Any basic sentence features a subject and a verb. For example, "I walked." When a person adds more words to it, they can indicate his/her feelings or personality. For example, I walked fast can indicate a sense of urgency, fear or insecurity. There are clear reasons why people specific words over others.

Similarly, there is a hidden meaning behind what people say. Through their choice of words people reveal emotions left unsaid.

Let's say you book a table to take your family out for dinner at one of the fanciest fine dines recently opened in your neighborhood. The server greets you courteously and directs you to your table. What follows is amazing dining experience.

The waiter introduces each of the seven courses in an informative yet engaging style, while you enjoy wining and dining in an upscale ambiance. After you enjoy a hearty meal and call for the tab, the waiter inquires if you enjoyed liked the food. You reply with, "The entrees were good."

The waiter doesn't look very delighted, though this appears to be a compliment on the face of it. These four words reveal your real opinion about the food. It implies that other than the entrees, everything else was pretty average or the only thing that stood out during the entire meal were the entrees.

Did you actually say everything else other than the entrees was average? No. Then, why did the waiter look crestfallen at your statement. It is obvious, people convey a lot not only through what they say but also through what they leave unsaid. Gather the hidden meaning or subtext behind what people say to tune in to their inner feelings. Notice how sometimes people will say, "you are looking lovely today." It can either mean you don't look plain everyday (which is a more passive aggressive kind of statement) or you are looking exceptionally good today compared to other days.

Another powerful clue about what people are thinking or feeling is noticing how they talk about other people. In a research published in the Journal of Personality and Social Psychology, helmed by Peter Harms and Siminie Vazire of the University of Nebraska and University of St. Louis respectively, it was discovered that merely asking participants to rate positive and negative traits of three person revealed a lot about the participant's social competence, general well-being, other people's perception of them and their mental health.

It was observed that an individual's inclination to view other people in a positive manner was a strong indication of their own positive emotions. There is a strong link between seeing others in a more positive light and being emotionally stable, happy, productive and enthusiastic.

On the other hand, viewing others in a negative light bears a strong correlation with a general sense of dissatisfaction, low self esteem, anti-social behavior and narcissism. People who hold plenty of negative emotions tend to perceive other people in a poorer or more negative light. This can also be an indication of emotional issues, mental health conditions or a personality disorder. Again, emotions aren't good or bad but a reflection of how you are feeling. If a person experiences more negative emotions for others around him/her, it can be a powerful clue to his/her emotions about himself/herself.

If a person says that they "made up their mind" after plenty of deliberation, the phrase indicates a mindset that is high on logic and rational thinking. The individual may be more contemplative and practical by nature. He/she may consider all the available options before making a decision. These are not your likely contenders for snap of the moment decisions.

Do you know what meta language is? It is the intended words behind the words you speak. You don't say something directly but reveal it through the words you use. For example, notice how when people want to get someone to agree to what they've said, they'll always place yes, done or okay followed by a question mark in the end. Like, I can't in the project today; I'll submit it tomorrow, okay? It is like manipulating the other person to agree.

To make your social emotional quotient even more powerful and impactful, pay attention to the sounds people utter other than coherent words. Moaning, grunting, sighing etc. can reveal a lot. Sometimes, these sounds will complement the words the speaker is using to make the message even more persuasive. However, at other times, there may be a mismatch between the person's words and sounds.

For example, someone may say, "I am having a really good day" followed by a sigh, which can indicate they are simply being sarcastic and are in fact having a bad day. The reading becomes more effective when you combine words and other miscellaneous speech sounds.

Environmental Clues

A person's immediate environment says a lot about their emotional state. For instance, a messy, unclean or disorganized space can indicate lack of clarity of emotions or thoughts. Of course everything has to be analyzed within a context. Someone may have an unkempt house because he/she is too busy to tidy it up and doesn't have housekeeping help. All of us have certain spaces around us that are inaccessible that we don't really bother cleaning or organizing (space behind the cupboard or under the bed). These are spaces that we wouldn't normally clean. If such spaces are immaculately clean or organized, it can indicate anxiety or a disorder (obsessive compulsive disorder).

Well-organized and clean spaces can indicate clarity of emotions or control over one's emotions. The person tends to be more reflective and introverted by nature. Similarly, people who are outwardly focused or extroverts tend to be surrounded by chaos.

This isn't pop psychology but based on clear principles of how the environment around us is created through our actions, which is directed by our subconscious thoughts and emotions. For example, using bright, vibrant and bold prints in your décor or attire can be a sign of confidence, emotional self-assurance, and independence of thought/ opinion. Likewise, a home with brighter and more vibrant colors is an indication is a sign of being bold, emotionally expressive and outgoing. These people are not afraid of taking risks and are more tuned into the needs and feelings of other people. More subtle colors imply inward directed emotions or an introverted personality. They may not be too clued in to other person's feelings and emotions.

People who hold on to old objects or hoard can be excessively emotional, sensitive or sentimental. They find it tough to move away their past emotions or are still ridden by feelings of shame, regret/guilt related to the past. These are people who latch on to old memories and are unable to release self limiting emotions that hold the back.

When you use these verbal and non verbal principles for understand people, your social emotional quotient invariably increases.

CONCLUSION

Congratulations, you've made it through to the end of Cognitive Behavior Therapy - The best techniques for overcoming depression, anxiety, and intrusive thoughts. Hopefully, it was able to provide you with helpful information to start taking control of your life and relationships. By applying the methods in this book, you should be able to make a significant change in your life when it comes to removing anxiety, depression, and negative thinking.

By understanding that our thoughts control our actions, we can start to change bad habits, recognize negative thought patterns, and heal our relationship with ourselves and others. Becoming aware of the different diagnosis for anxiety and depressive disorders can help us to identify our own mental health issues and develop goals so that we can handle our feelings and actions. To get the most out of Cognitive Behavior Therapy, we must be willing to discuss our feelings and emotions honestly. Work on setting clear expectations for yourself and put in the work it will take to reach your goals.

You can change your situation by losing any victim mentality you may have. Listen to your body and mind and give yourself the space needed to make positive impacts physically, mentally, emotionally, and spiritually. Remember to breathe and be gentle with yourself. Practice filtering out negative thoughts and replacing them with reasonable ones. Take a realistic assessment before, during, and after your cognitive behavioral therapy sessions and use them as a roadmap to where you want to be. You should soon start to feel more in control of your thoughts, emotions, and your life!

Copyright © 2019 Daniel Stevens
All rights reserved.

www.ingramcontent.com/pod-product-compliance
Lightning Source LLC
Chambersburg PA
CBHW062158290526
45791CB00016B/1154